My Little Book
of Exiles

My Little Book of Exiles

DAN ALTER

THE **BLACK SPRING**
PRESS GROUP

First published in 2021
Eyewear Poetry, an imprint of
Eyewear Publishing Limited, The Black Spring Press Group
Grantully Road, Maida Vale, London W9,
United Kingdom

Typeset with graphic design by Edwin Smet
Author photograph Adrianne Mathiowetz
Cover collage Edwin Smet

The right of Dan Alter to be identified as author of
this work has been asserted in accordance with section 77
of the Copyright, Designs and Patents Act 1988

ISBN 978-1-913606-94-7

Editor's note: the author has requested that American spelling and grammar be used in this work.

BLACKSPRINGPRESSGROUP.COM

To the labor of mothers:
my own, who started me on my way;
Jess, who brought me home.

CONTENTS

after days
of what translated
strangely

FOREFATHERING

I came in from Romania, it was raining
like the whole country was smoking.
From Poland, ground that would say a million

times no. Russia, ruining its own soil
in flecked sunlight all the way
to the Urals, blew out the candles

on our birthday cakes. Russia was always
at our backs & I came in small enough
to be knocked down easily by boys

who wore tiny reminders of their god
dying. Tinging like the handlebar bell,

my two wheels stable only in motion.

Left a mother & her kinds of words,
oaky centuries of snow & whispered babies
down the well. All my nine brothers

vacated, sisters faded under the gray
from Moscow, in the name of the worker,
choked. Beard-shave became shoe-shine,

put hands under hoods of the new motors,
between wars I had some taxis
but that went away. Dollar down,

dollar up, my tongue inflected,
my two children turned west,

as we listened to gasoline singing.

You wake up to the rain.
Your rhythm hollowed like a snare. You
can't find me, busy

becoming air. I look out your eyes
onto another world: skinny strings of rain,

steady & small like applause.

HILLS & BAY, THROUGH A VIEWMASTER C. 1969

My father was driving a truck
full of paragraphs:
in their boxes, elegant.
Mom came back from long

walks in a cemetery no-one
else could see. The swimming pool

we filled with pain,
it rippled. On the spiral

staircase of our DNA the whole family

halted before the panoramic
plunge of hillside to bayshore,

crawl of antmobiles. Our cats
lurked around developing
their wordless vendettas: I mistook

my sister for one as she stalked me
in the dark. Through walls

you could hear feral music.

In the fog's bleed-off, whistling
my father left chapters
at a closed door, mom

over burners opened
her mouth but only graveyard

came out. Miracles of birth having

given way to a light drizzle
for decades, mathematics
unraveled in the cheat-grass,

two plus two in reverse. He rose
like smoke rings. In her despair

we went into the sunny coastal afternoon

to see through chlorine how long
could we hold our breath—

LABOR POEM #9

Student Services Newsletter, Oberlin OH

From my shoulder bag, the sidewalks, the bright,
the stillness of. Dorm, dining hall leave five,
bite of frozen air. But my breath. Is this,
the pedals' wobbly, the reflective snow,
doorway. Of air on my cheeks. The looming
stillness of the dorm. Is this what. The pink sheets
three or five. Dark glass door and when it swings.
Coaster brakes, bright reflective stillness
of snow. Is this. From my shoulder, the sheets.
The looming, but my breath, an office and some-
one in a turtleneck. Dorm leave four or three
printed sheets, chestnut, kelly green, is this
what life is. The library door, dark glass.
The bright, the bite of. My breath. And when it swings.

TATTERED WHITE FLAG

In the juicer of the soul   no fruit   Who knows
the straight path to turn words into money   Fence
covered with passionflower   a hummingbird I'm

strung between   Never learned the rules of dominos
but I made them fall in a row   Raise your tattered
white flag   Struggle struggle   the muscle of my heart

If they're tired they don't let on   working
in calibrated buildings to convert
the remaining drops of rainwater to money

For how many lifetimes do we make the same
mistake Again Jacob's sons sell their brother
In the meantime   cirrus   bicycles   cup of tea

steeped all day   Should I apologize   None of us
succeeded   we fail bravely like Noah   There's
no umbrella big enough for that kind of rain

ON BEING UNABLE TO SEE THE CAREER OF BENJAMIN ZUSKIN EXCEPT THROUGH THE LENS OF HIS EXECUTION IN ONE OF STALIN'S PURGES

For a while the revolution had a use for its minorities.
30 years of curtains, romance of proscenium air through

which his lines. But 49 bound volumes
of charges: *The ground is burning beneath my feet*

he whispered to a visitor. Proscenium thrust forward
in Yiddish by that century as it developed out of the barrel

of various guns. From Ponievezh Lithuania a mostly Jewish
town to Moscow, born the same year as my own grandfather but

instead went east. Absences casting shadows, from the first
state sponsored runs wasn't the gun always on stage?

Can I from my remove see the audience fading into fear,
hear language as it was erased, secret police taking him

asleep on a gurney to his finale of interrogation, 49
bound volumes. Special delivery of his stage partner's death

under truck wheels. When a visitor from somewhere safer
asked what message to convey, he whispered.

Can I feel where they scissored through his papers,
from here I'm combing my hair with someone's death.

MY LITTLE BOOK OF EXILES

Crickets   crickets   blur the dark
fields   our car divides by miles per
how many hours

As ocean travel fades
from memory   so the feeling
after weeks   when they saw dry land

All night while I moved out
of you   your eyes on one star
in a window   among windows   Manhattan's millions

of tons   island where no-one said who
for their bows   had gathered hickory
driven like pollen drifts west   & west

In my Book of Exiles always
you   driving away from your child
on roads paved with leaving

with longing for more land
Up in skinny branches of a backyard
pine I seemed to be

the earth's last person

People I come from when you
got here   was the ground you left
already closing like skin

GATES

1. Arches

Sha'ar p'takh dodi, he wrote, near the year one
thousand, in Saragossa, despairing in the citrus
and pools of a walled courtyard, his Israel calls:
open the gate, my love, get up and open—

eight lines locking like arches around the grief
of exile. As in: Cordova, the sound of a door
leaning into the air, cindered, after his people fled
the *Juderia*, his father among them. *Open the gate*:

2. State Developmental Center, Stockton, CA

The smell of the halls, a floor soap only used in the buildings
where people are discarded: like a decaying body layered with
perfume. Vinyl tile flooring, painted concrete-block walls;
the aggressive scent following us to her ward. A heavy steel
door, wire-mesh laces the viewing-glass. Against which, first
to respond to the buzzer's abrasion, two or three of their faces
press: wet with drool or mucous, eyes thick, mouths askew. As
soon as the orderly with the ring of keys lets us in, they close
around us. They talk over each other, repeating their five- or
two-word stories, trying to meet our eyes.

3. God heard

For my spirit is terrified, is taken with shaking:
like grasses in the roadside wind, or scarves
of kelp winding in tide. *God heard the other
boy's cry,* wrote Ibn Gabirol, and wandered

to Granada. *In deep midnight I am chased by the wild ass,*
run over by the forest boar. His words would go on,
copied, sung, while he lay down on a stone floor. Valencia,
asking, please let me out, or, into—

4. State Developmental Center

The ward waiting room. Wall-mounted televisions,
fluorescence, and more of them on shabby couches, staring
or shuffling here to there on the checker-board floor. And
her scarred, doughy, patched face, some drained color of
sweatsuit hanging bagged on her body. Her broken-toothed
grin.

Her years behind this door or ones like it. Brain clogged with
the tiny growths, marbled with anti-convulsants, pinned
down to one thought, of a family thirty years ago, still under
one roof. On every visit my sister asks, when can she come
back.

5. Harbor

Open up the gate, my love, get up and open—

Saragossa, which sounds like wind
in grass, or stone walls, mossy,
sounds like the ocean's brush on sand:
it has charged up the shore, is receding.

TRACES

Then I was mostly scared   & mostly the house was
spiders   stringing seasons   into fog through which
sometimes a record played   someone singing

My father's father went door to door the rest
of his life selling brushes hearing no Romanian
he wore out his ears with roar of his Buick

The Danube River Delta   Black Crowned Night Heron
Greylag Goose White Pelican   320
species of birds I can google but what use

is a grandfather I met two or three times
The traces make the sound of dust   one mind
by itself   wind in leaves & litter

Violins in complete dark of their cases
Houses left alone have come through into daylight
carrying air left empty or used up

PAUL'S AMERICA

Needle down, lead-in groove clicks, steel-strung waltz
volumes out of wood cabinets.

Country of their humming:

baseline in descent, throaty guitar
and organ pirouettes at fade-out—

warm as skin, two men's voices

blended and rising like smoke.

The song proposed an America

of no Richard Nixon nor shot-down

JFK, neither burning

Detroit nor carpet-bombed Cambodia—

notwithstanding

its release date, a single

day before the Reverend Dr. dropped

on a Memphis balcony; but rather,

of a gentile girl, a Greyhound out of Michigan,

a slight hope for the two of them,

strung across their distances in a necklace

of dactyls: an America where a thronged

      Times Square or arm-linked

            thousands on the Mall—fade

to just these two. The one—

      eyes closed, the other aching

            out the window, streaked with headlights.

Paul Simon's almost-hymn on which I

      rose up from wall to wall

            carpet, over shingled

rooftops, past the snow-draped

      trees to mix with radio waves

            and sparrows, massed in migration,

his America which lingers still in the vinyl turns

      per minute opening my 1982

            living room into a highway—

I too came to look for it, and saw

      that it was sad, that the promise of a trip

            into-the-sunset would not redeem it,

that very promise bused across

      the rural miles, Kathy

            stepping off again to buy smoke

and pastries, and always

      falling asleep. Oh and that's when

            he pours out his heart.

I WAS ALSO ONE OF THE BOYS OF SUMMER

I came back to play baseball when it was already getting cool.
The ball was drifting, up over voices.
Coach on the once-white bench, the crack tuned
right into my ears. As they say, summer fades,
the boys of summer fold up like accordions,
wishing they could roll up the fields and carry them,
saying honey, play that song again you know the one.
Now we know that the world's not a simple place,
while you stretch for a high throw someone steals,
or you're turning for your name and the team's gone.

No hit for weeks, team gone, I'm grown.
And then she wants to hold my hand, standing
the way I was, composing to the fly-ball's arc.
And she says no, new game, where we walk in
and you buy me a cone of sweet pink cotton.
But I was just prepared to bring the bat around
like a screen door springing shut to keep
the cold out. We stand by the car a long time arguing—

but the crowd shouts were thin things, wisps in the sugary air,
only white balls bouncing solitary towards you,
only the chubby coach's protection by the leaning of his heart
from the bench. When both teams shook hands,
late sunlight, lazy shoes, play ball boys, summer's
almost over, before you know it, the chill is in, grass's
green dries down to a whisper, but I came back
to play baseball, I was also one of those runners,
a tight-suited part of the living net
that shifted, not to let the ball get through.

ODE TO GROWING UP TEN YEARS TOO LATE

Buckskin vest on a bare chest
the blonde-maned impresario hippie
rides believe it or not a white
horse! across the aftermath where others
also unshirted pick through trash
for the burning. Half a million
young have by now dragged their come
down bodies into mini-buses
to struggle down a long mountain
of disappointment. I have seen. I get
my records in the dollar bin. The star
spangled feedback has died away
& the left hand that plied it.
It has dawned on me that there will be
no more Beatles albums no more
that the near past has already
been the moment we were
waiting for. Now we are waiting
it out in reverse. At one of my mother's
seminars under the baffled lights I was
instructed to make in the sky
behind closed eyes a peace
room where duly I set sun-colored
fish to swim in a glass floor.
But never fed them.

Oh spirit of acid,
you have become something
in the rain. Somewhere in Queens
to a very fast count of four a man
who has reinvented his last name
begins to sing
I wanna be sedated.

ODE TO MY LOST VIRGINITY

While semis went somewhere
through Pennsylvania in diesel
glare   & John Lennon
not long in the ground with his
eyes that were always off-
focused on love
                              You
who had come the whole
way with me like a raincoat
of cellophane   who were
loyal while I broke empties
against a neighborhood
backstop in the dark
            who had stayed after I wished
you'd go having learned
of a place I couldn't take you

            did not even protest when a girl
within minutes understood
& brought me to a worn clearing
to let our bodies slide down
the hill bodies come from

Did you wander into the woods
tripping on undergrowth blind
now that my eyes were not
with you
                              The blueness
behind black sky came down
future rang once
or twice a doorbell to what

turned out to be many
empty rooms
                  the call of life
to itself ebbed sticky
in the dirt   I wasn't listening
I will return and stay
longer I promised staring
at pinholes in a cooling
universe   she
humoring me the way they do

          Is that when you
slipped like a balloon
released
          were you seen
years later resurfacing
in traffic as a glance
between slowly rolling cars
both radios playing

LABOR POEM # 1

Wisconsin State Journal, Madison WI

The baskets, handlebars, the back tire swerve.
Light snow over in the dark. The back tire
over the light, the load. And a little
after 5 am the heavy baskets, hill.
All my trouble rolled down. Cold fingers,
the paper load, gloves only partly. The rolled
and the rolled. Taped handlebars, apartment dark
rows. For my trouble, rubber band, a dog,
the heavy baskets. Deliver and deliver.
Alarms they have not yet heard. Fingers in
the cold gloves only partly. All my trouble
to deliver. The swerve, a dog. Snow back tire
over after 5 am. The basket load down
a light snow hill, my trouble in the dark.

FOG OVER ASHKENAZ

Could I have come from nowhere
Ancestors' ground a floating zone between countries

called the Pale   or was that from the shade of their skin
in Christian shadows   My father's eyes

come from names I've tried to learn   & lost

1100 years of sojourning can't be wrong   but my four
grandparents among the lucky enough
to leave before   The trouble I'm starting out in

a gap that widens   In the swallowing whole was it all
lost   or did their spirit filter to points the letters
mark   a hole I'm looking into   Yiddish

speakers in shade of black forests   Somewhere near

say Vilna their feet must have touched ground   Alter
meaning elder in Yiddish   which is sticky with
11th Century German   what haven't you lost

of their art   Fog is general all over Ashkenaz
In minutes the shtetl names have drifted   Wouldn't

I feel a whole lot better not rummaging
for origins in that tight a crawlspace   Still

five layers of shade make the skin paler

than fog   Yes it ended badly but my father
didn't get his blue eyes from nowhere

A NIGHT AT THE OLD MARKETPLACE

In *A Night in the Old Marketplace*, the two leading men of the Moscow State Jewish Theater emcee at a wedding of a dead bride to a groom who has crawled out of an offstage grave. As have their guests. She has a worm embedded in her cheek.

But it's only 1928.

The part about the dead comes after shadowy figures of the living have chorused across the stage set with houses leaning in untenably. Children calling into shadows of children, prostitutes, an old drunk named Nosn. Klezmer musicians who had drowned in the town well. Old men arguing with God. When it plays in Vienna, even Freud is moved to come backstage.

Zuskin and Mikhoels, in the doubled part of *badkhen* lead the ghoul celebrations. Morning comes to end *A Night*, nothing having happened except the dead coming back to life, the way of life from which they come being played dead, a generation ahead of schedule.

Look at them, propped on each other, hands proffered at angles. Old photograph dissolving in each direction of light.

ROOMS FOR THE LIVING

Museum plaza she waits an hour on grass
to get her face painted   butterflies
in lines for the day of the dead

So far how many ways are you dying
I carry my water everywhere   Come
stay   there's living rooms too

In her basket my daughter has a twig   toothpicks
a fingernail-size screwdriver   Dan you'll
be washing dishes long after you're dead

In the hills above my father's white hair grows
recklessly   When I'm this tired   is it the dead
I'm half in the way of

Yellow strained cloud shade   on concrete stairs
memories' tread & rise   If you see me twisting
it's the downed   branches I can't   not step on

CANT

i

Dead as dust Ezra

took down a bottle   & poured two

glasses   His eyes in Rapallo sunlight
         alternating

between sea   & slate

As I drank my inside

was exposed

Onto bare

floors light spilled

off the sea   I smiled

too much

His eyes ghost
blue
or sand blank

ii

He was leaving just
as I got here I think

it was snowing though
it could have been ash flaking

in Italy I would come
to know his mind as it splintered

across the page white
with a force he spent his life

in the library gathering   it's snowing
on stains on stone pavement

& angles of awning   I understand
it doesn't snow in the real

Rapallo a southern vacation town
but it does in this poem because

I want to bury him in his own white

everyone makes excuses
him pinned in the US Army cage

or mesmerized by sea-surge
his ear for Homer in breakers

on pier posts   poor as a graveyard rat

iii

On your way across the end
of a thousand years scavenging

for baskets of whatever gleamed
things inside you grew like pale

grass under a house sometimes
they sounded like money sometimes a voice

proliferating into voices pitched
to a scream you wanted to leave

monuments to live in them
so that in the middle of lines

pivoting in air containers
of something distilled sunlit

your mouth became part of a hole
which not far away many of the kind

of people I come from
fell into   I don't want

to hate you still the whitening
past you spent your life on

is falling

STATE OF THE ATMOSPHERE

At 8 am white people hurry towards bad weather
garbage trucks dominate the street   I lose
my race with differences in the air

Generation raised on Homer Simpson
the unanimous yoga pose
all in trouble with the weather

David Bowie flared   but also faded
back into the background   station lights flicker
past   then the shaking dark underground

Behind muscular glass chimpanzees watch us
think about ourselves   at this point
in September   California's all tinder

Baudelaire's poems drift away & he had no
deodorant   I'm just saying   what was I thinking
going out the door in sweatpants this morning

These fights we have   when I wash the dishes
do I mind enough the knife blade   child snoring
resentment   the fire-weather we're bent around

PURGATORY FOR POUND

I have stationed you down
                    stairs in soil
        of Europe
your train
                not coming   the tracks
        too busy   with theirs

Consider the apparition of these
        faces   cousins even
                of your friend
        many times removed
                                They are
your cage   gray toned
        boys   grandmothers
                        in head scarves all below
        ground damp

Their eyes   sea green
        or brown
                around centers light can't
        return from   are petals
plucked by an imagination
                into which
        yours merged

No it won't   cohere
        an injury you let
                                lodge in print
                The faces
are still crowding off cars
                        into your dark
        your dark
                is wet & black
                        Bow

LABOR POEM #6

Tractor delivery route, Kibbutz Gesher Haziv

But I failed at the curve. The perimeter
fence, the windbreak trees. To back up. The wheels,
how fast on a dirt road. The loading dock, fresh
from the chicken house, dust motes of mid after-
noon. The bulk of laundry bags, stacked cylinders
of the children's meals, chicken house. Down around
the curve. To back up with a trailer, the front
wheels. Fresh eggs, stacked, the wheels which way, or you
jackknife it. Mid afternoon, the bulk of,
with a trailer to the loading dock. Bags, stacked
cylinders, the perimeter skid, the wheels,
failed. Down around, on a dirt road how fast does
a tractor. A section of fence. Down. The wind-
break trees. Dust motes. A trailer, which way the wheels.

ODE TO THE IDEA OF FRANCE

Because life is too filled with failures, shins
banged, shoes that no sooner
home from the store don't fit,
once more in the doorway turning
back but the words, only magnets
drawing metal fury. I have hidden
and hidden my hopes, slipped free
of their knots ragging my skin until I am
my own Houdini, escaping the handcuffs
and glass-walled water-closet
of my self. My first car, for instance,
was an ancient Ford Falcon van with no seats
in back, just carpet, bought from a lady
in a parking lot to bus my friends
every weekend to the beach, which we did,
more or less, once. And my friends
who had held to each other like the inflated
raft after a plane crash, floated off. So
let there be France! not the one we can visit,
with universal healthcare and five weeks
off every year, saturated with museum
tickets, baguettes and stinky cheese
next to the Seine sun down; nor the one
that with gusto packed its Jews onto trains
for the solution to the east, nor France
of the banned hijab, car burnings
spreading from rage in the suburbs;
                              but a someday France
across the unsullied water where the Paris commune
sheds its light into history, where the evening
mist is tender on country fields, and pizzicato
continues an orchestra into the gentle

summer dark. A France of sensible little cars
but still enough headroom, of movies
about people like us stumbling
back toward happiness, France
of bison in ochre motion on cave walls
at the end of the last ice age, where I can drop
the recent centuries to the floor like my shirt,
can undo the zip ties of our suffering
and make up right then.

                    This is not, I know, convincing.
The Antarctic ice-sheets really are
dissolving. Oh my friends, demoralized,
medicated and spread everywhere like margarine,
like you, I do not know what to do.

to call
the world
by its secret name

*We, who have been uprooted, must first learn to know the soil
and prepare it for our transplantation… We, who have been torn
away from nature… if we desire life, we must establish a new
relationship with nature, we must open a new account with it.*
AD Gordon *c. 1920*

16 ARLOSOROFF STREET

Flowers from the corner market
the year of that famous
handshake on the white
house lawn I was living
on the third floor just down
the street from the Prime Minister's
residence everywhere the Jerusalem-stone
facades flowers for Friday and I
felt sure I had found the eyes
I was looking for
the tall blond President's arms
out while the Chairman and ex-general
signed and even took
each other's hand
daily the protesters waved placards
wild-eyed down the street
and after all night with her
walking the hewn city
steps we kissed on the green-
draped balcony the same limestone
facades broke the mountain
light back I thought
forever kissed just
once or twice it wasn't
going to work but I loved to get
flowers from the corner though
I didn't learn their names and sometimes
also in Hebrew a newspaper
it looked like peace
might have come

COMING IN FROM THE COLD

(Ode to Uprising, Track 1)

down a gravel road in a run-down
cabin in June we listen continually
to the final album Bob Marley
made & him only a month
dead of melanoma we join
every echo of the ladies
chirping backup follow the lilt
& rubber pulse the acrobatic
rasp of his voice nothing
has prepared me for how many people
can fit inside the sparse room
of this music & I have

opened my mother's next
screen door to boys who will take me
into their rooms & show me album
covers sinuous with limbs I will find
myself as if sleep-walked onto a mat
to be pinned & will accept
nicknames you might call a symptom

so when I step into a smattering of maples
& shaggy grass for the ingathering
of the exiles of Skokie Ann Arbor
Detroit I am entirely un-
prepared for the canvas shade
dust-bombed couches where we turn up
all the way the Wailers'
understated beat & is it
really a surprise we don't mourn
the singer's early death he has

come into our world with all the acid
sweet of a pineapple if you never
tasted one & then a first bite

ZION TRAIN

(Ode to Uprising, Track 6)

AD Gordon for instance was the father figure
the rest of them just kids who fought
with their parents crowded into sweaty
Yiddish meetings shipped
to Palestine to conduct
affairs with bee hives there was
word of a worker's state
it was a time to stop
praying for rain and make the rain
out of dirt everything would be
made out of it Fridays they
would wear white peasant
shirts slightly embroidered
would have candles
as eyes muscles like Picasso
masks the reclaimed grain
would spread with their
Van Gough calluses
selfishness would melt

we finger-dampened our mimeographed
excerpts of the father figure
in the cities of Reagan profit
was pumping up we hid out
the summer in rural Michigan
Zion Train was coming
our way if that's not what
the Rastafarian meant how did he know
about us how we dressed
the Midwestern grass in ideas
of going home the flower edged

shirt that sea shimmering
the original blue
no streets there only
footpaths it couldn't
be too late

LABOR POEM #2

Banana Plantation, Kibbutz Gesher Haziv

I crouched down. The leaf and the dried leaf. Not
a machete, more of a chef's knife. Alone
in the row. The dried, the rotting, the leaf.
The sap. Thought I saw a tarantula,
me or someone else. Stains. Alone, after
a week, a book that I tried, or someone else
ahead in the next row. Not romantic after
a week. The sap stains, the slice at the base. Not
trees, a prehistoric grass. A book I tried
to think about. The rotting between the trees,
not trees. I crouched down. Chef's knife, stains, everything
brown. The next row, leaf, a tarantula
under, me or someone else, the next. A book
I tried, everything brown. Not after a week.

WAYS OF SAYING

After days of what translated   strangely as congress   a hundred
odd kids like us   in a dining hall pouring words

both typed up & spoken   into always larger spaces made
by our longings   for a not realized world

it seemed like some knowing   one of the other had already
been in rain & mud-ruts   of a Lithuania when she & I sat across

a table paper-clothed white   in the story of a sundown's loan
of extra souls   & I heard her voice's   several rivulets

summer was dissolving   & us collected from camps named
for rises   or plains in a distance where imagination

gathered   years   later in Lake Kaiser between faded
rope floats I had another   chance because of life

guard class a few days   until buses unloaded into our
care the even younger than us   in its opaque green lakeness how lucky

I felt the murky squish of her   slippery against my own
cold torso or learning   in a nearby night

field a fugue in turn   of last century Hebrew
באופל ליל *ask the stars where   is their light* but by when

our breaths iced I was   trying as a way of keeping
head above what came   spilling up to force open

a door she seemed   to have locked   the other
day across an ocean she   said how Hebrew has so many

words for longing   always wanting to call the world   by its secret name

REDEMPTION SONG

(Ode to Uprising, Track 10)   *for B.B.*

how much redemption could a song contain
every weekend you drove
your gas guzzler three hours to stare
into the eyes of a girl
on her parent's sofa minutes
until someone gave & how directly
sad you were your despair gave off
a gray light we knew next
to nothing about Pan-Africanism
or the lyrics lifted
from Marcus Garvey but we
recognized the buzzback of that
one tinny string in the bass-line
awkward like us

when Bob's smoke-
stained thumbnail plucked
the low strings you followed
he sang *captivity* you
saw school cinderblock
emancipate you pointed
yourself upward from cold
drugstore aisles or exhaust-
snow ragging the roadside

your sadness alloyed with something
unsubmitting the way you laced
your hashbrowns with tabasco
& made of them a victory you lost
patience tuning but when you
took up the assuredness of that

melody how it returns to its own
shore you had something
to drive half a day for
though 3 minutes 49 could
only take us so far

YOU ONLY KNOW IT BY ITS DOUBLE-NOTE

From that road you couldn't see trains. Poles bearing
the high & low voltages, muffled roar of miles
my wheels erased, while I was driving towards warm.

A night tracing skin under her sweatshirt was
the world days erased. Winter approaching, blowy
Chicago kept its distance, from that far does it

matter she & I finished almost as soon as
started? Miles of time have blurred her sorry
but no. Memory wants an opening.

Chicago was open in the past we could touch.
With a telephone from my room, which was
smaller until it was erased. Wasn't I free?

I think I'm starting over, but it's over again.
As free as telephone poles from their tree,
loaded with cables over rooftops, rooftops.

Two or one nights doesn't add up to what we
raced toward, I'm starting over. Outside trains
loaded with a past you can't see, exactly.

We met around a warmth like planets. Around us
Chicago wheeled & folded its fields up, trains
rolled distance as if it could be erased.

Another time I lay in her bed feeling it
was love calling me to Chicago, driver
of a car full of the past I couldn't arrive to

or erase like snow whiting out fields. Or take
again, or carry away like a train you
only know from its double-note in the distance—

AND THEN YOU DRAW BAD CARD

(Ode to Uprising, track 3)   *for P.B.*

how did you already know
about the 15 minutes trapped
in traffic dream the circus dance of all
the friends at the end of 8 ½ or also
in black & white that silhouetted
line of them dancing after Death
in the Seventh Seal & even
the light-footed early Woody
staging his own joke Dance
of Death on a pull-down screen
for a dollar every Friday night
that fall the startled world
unfolding for us merely by taking
the downtown bus & diagonal
tree-lined paths onto campus
while the brunt of winter
accrued beyond us there was
your slight touch at my elbow &
displaced giggle in another
decade fingernails painted
black & strung out
on anti-somethings you
pursuing another soulmate by
was it train to Waukesha would be
in a lobby handcuffed while you were
just drumming on a glass
top table but that
was the future poison
stories of Woody & daughter had
not yet come
after the final flicker-out

of credits we stepped
down a windy slopeful
of architecture towards night's
last bus I was swept through
with you my
life just coming open

LABOR POEM #8

Royal Pacific Fisheries, Kenai Alaska

His trailer up. The salt air and damp, the old
barge moored. Rust-colored paint, coils. John the foreman,
from his time, styrofoam. The sheds, the hull, paint
everything metal. My cup of red. Paint
against the salt, corrosive. Coils of rope or
hose, the days between. A story from his time
in the navy, his trailer up, the instant
coffee in styrofoam. Rope or hose, you
stretch out long. Cooling. Everything metal,
rust-colored. And damp, my cup of red tea
cooling. Stretch it out, twist as you throw each
coil down. Up on the beach, the barge moored, the days
between. Corrosive. The paint against. The instant
in styrofoam. You twist, throw each coil down.

TOMATOES, SUMMER'S FIRST

And this one is for Michigan, for her latticed rivers, for her fire-
    flies tickering the dark which is made of muslin, which
    cloaks the lush of her long grasses.
And this one is for an M, met yesterday, at campfire, steel
    strings and voices leaning in a Saturday evening,
for her jacket which has fluttered down denim onto so skinny
    shoulders,
and for canoeable rivers which scud down from Canada to fill
    the mother lake,
and also for the temerity of the fireflies, which are blinking
    orange mini-blimps.
And this is for her fingers, humming in the damp of my palm,
    and this one is for patrolling night-watch
in Michigan, the evening melted, pointillistic, separating into a
    fizz, into the splash and spill of M talking.

And how, in an unused cabin with cloudy moonlight slivering,
    her mouth floated to my mouth,
and this is for kissing on the squeak of cot springs, behind the
    whisk of screen door,
and this for that door, for its sad belly, humidity-aching hinges,
    on it the yearning mosquitoes arrayed,
for her mouth which was kind and placed me in a room full of
    sugar bursting, flashing in my body which had been dark,
that was the sweep of her friendliness, slipping away to spit out
    sour and my fingers sent from elastic of panties.
And this is for panties on the untouched crotch then of M,
    maybe blue as a Kalamazoo sky, or pink as baby bottom
    under diaper,
but were no color for me, their worn cotton thread count kept
    within jeans and skin I tried to be nice to.

Also for the jeans jacket, metal stiff of its buttons, its hint of
     men on horseback, how it meant to make us feel older
     than we were.
And M, at a pause in our walk, in the cavernous kitchen where
     mops hang crusting, under blue light of bug zappers,
among the suspended pots I will always gaze at you through my
     eyes with the filters off,
only two nights for us, tapping on the bruised aluminum bellies
     of saucepans,
you spinning a future we wouldn't have, talking us off to a mar-
     ket stall in Mexico, where we would never
buy salad, and how we would know the flushed taste of toma-
     toes at summer's first bursting.

And this is finally for M, stepping through a creak screen door
     swinging back on where she had spit,
for pinecones of kindness on cabin shading branches, for five
     fingers slightly sweaty,
for voices braided with folk song, swallowed by night, and then
     morning
coming with all the opened doors swung back shut, but the shut
     ones smiling
taking their places back in the single-file procession of time,
     with firefly maple-tops and dark-swaddled Junegrasses,
washed in the webbing of rivers running from ice ages endlessly
     down to their lake.

MAKE IT WORK

(Ode to Uprising, track 5)   for D.S.

if anyone could have it seemed
to be you the guy almost
immune to what made
the rest of us hesitate
at 14 already gone
to see what the high
flown talk of land
& labor was about
sent me a soft faced
snapshot yourself under one
of your Hebrew cows

but Evanston doesn't
really border Beit Alfa the age
of heroes a hundred
years over & post-
school last stands
of the road trip not-
withstanding we didn't *come together*
& make it work
                    instead scattered
on a street named for a Judean
commander the Romans
I would later learn threw
from a cliff you handed me
another stack of warmed over
Woody we had come
too late to hop
freight trains but you
pulled up to my Oakland
curb with Ben & a full
tank & opened
your minivan door

COULD YOU BE LOVED
(Ode to Uprising, Track 8)

back home each of us the last
one left at the flecked
formica table our mothers
tried to serve us something we
would like but we had put on
headphones
                    say something Bob
in the hit single keeps
turning to plead or order
an unnamed someone to answer
back that made sense
for us our mothers waited
in the dark called through
the screen door the smell
of smoke their marriages
over we had already
passed through them

afternoons unhappy
in sweat suit I circled
a short blonde among others
working with pom poms
while I ran never
learning her name
                    could you be
could you be my mother
all evening at her desk your
mother's voice a door
slamming lipstick applied
over the bitterness
the women who kept fridge

stocked for us were for us
wilted we were always not calling
looking off into lighter-
flamed stadium or the humming
tubes of Greyhound
terminal while they waited
their bedside lamps
still lit on piles of books
titled *Passages* & *Women*
Who Love Too Much

AMERICA, PROPOSAL
with Paul Simon

I tuned, I strung and spread apart the chord trying to unlock it, to let us
be carried up over rooftops like the painted lovers, because to be lovers
was what we were always driving toward. I dialed, to say we'll marry
our way past their divorces, would meet in air and throw our fortunes
in the trunk. Borrowed cars. The dotted lines stitching our cities together.

Then it was rest stops, it was white stripes, it was me not saying I've got
a mind churned with all of a sudden, with turnpike. It was her silences, some real
holes in the weather in the car. Cassettes and headlights to cover darkness, the state,
summer rain, someone's musty lake house. Here
she said, we lay down on couches. But still the road-motion in my
shivering, in our stares, in how by morning her bag
was already packed and shoulder-slung. So

what if I lost, phone number fumbled, after we bought
blank tapes to fill with music love letters, thin as a pack
of cards, unlucky as a smoker losing her war with cigarettes?
And what if no call back, and never saw after, and Mrs.
someone else had her somewhere life with a Tom or Wagner, pies
blue-lighted in the diner window, evening drive home? And
still couldn't stop thinking about it, as we walked off
from then, spread apart and left to look
in face after passing face for a glimpse, for
something placed inside memory like a car-trunk and driven all across America.

LABOR POEM #5

Polyziv, plastic shipping pallets, Kibbutz Gesher Haziv

Headphones. The whole night, injection mold roar
and squeal. The floating black pallets. Every few
weeks the whole night. Ben says. Machine roar, stack
for the foreman. And squeal, machine, but
the headphones, plastic injection. Break at 3
AM, margarine. Headphones, the whole night
floating black. Toast at 3 am, foreman
on his forklift. My roommate Ben says he
dances. Floating, the machine roar, headphones
all the way. Every few weeks walking back
with sunrise. Spread thin. The pallets stack.
The stack, foreman on his forklift. Dances, he
says. My roommate Ben. The sunrise walking.
But the headphones, plastic, all the way up.

POEM WITH DISHES & DEAD SEA

Sun going   she showed him
how to wash the whole

sinkful with half the water   sun
gone   So much

was new   Desert residue
went leaking from the helter-skelter

Jerusalem-stone houses   In the dark
he was swollen with her body's

words   pillow trickle hum

Voices runneled from windows
piled up on all sides   She held

a hand toward him in kindness
while her eyes continued to the humid

valley   onion fields   vines
raising fruit up trellises in rows

full of distance   Her friends   also older
took their last sparkling sentences

away to sleep   From kitchens of triple
exiled Kurdish Jews   air dusted

with crushed seeds & pepper
passed their courtyard on its way

down barrens to the lowest place
on earth

                    By morning
on the table a torn open

sheet of the feather-thin blue

paper they had once used to fly
what they felt around the world

JERUSALEM, FROM INCREASING DISTANCES

She wanted him to write her from the last seat of the bus, from the motion of warm northern wind along a lake shore, from the vanishing he kept in his backpack, from the bruised blue evening of his summer job. From the curved landscape of lettering, reportedly mystical city of the past. She wanted him to gather all the departure in his arms, to collapse it, to enclose it in envelopes back to her. She was not at the station, but her letters kept finding him in changing leaves and more generous water. Her letters kept peeling layers off the future of his skin. Her letters kept appearing in the distant weather, landing in his hands as saveable as rain.

WALKING BY THE LAKE,
AFTER STUDYING TORAH

And Jacob woke from his sleep and said… this is the gateway to the sky.
—*Genesis 28:16-17*

From days inside as if
underwater light, the worked
tissue of verses: onto a lake

trail, into almost snow. Collapsed
cattail husks, bare willow,
a wooden ladder drifts up

through the straying branches. Time
slowed down by the quiet almost
until we're holding our

breath. Here in a spot with oil
on the stones, ice skin on little
puddles, a glitter surprised on the ground.

THE BIGGEST THING THERE WAS THE SKY

I have also loved bicycles my body
upright through the air wheels too
mostly air the secure of derailleur
click the legs' work speaking
to the world and especially
how without falling
the banking over into a turn
a short ride away a slight
nineteen-year-old her mouth elastic
with feeling underlined the important
sentences in my flat
Ohio town the quietness
of the bicycles more than cars there

one night she was going
to die in my dream I burst
open as she told me
it was a spokes-and-sky
town through elm
and maple streets shedding
and later among the night-
glow of snowbanks her face
felt like one of the wide
screened-in porches in that town
full of clouds where I also
loved a weathered one-speed

when I woke she
who had other places in mind
was still alive my two
wheels raced through
a town full of clouds like a cloud

garden ribbony crimsons and oranges
also loose in air edging
on winter one-speeding to behold
her what color were
her eyes she always said
hi like she was handing
you a ripe berry

LABOR POEM #15

Subway Guitars Bicycles, Berkeley CA

Kickstands and the grease caked on. The spokes, grease,
gaps in the spoke lace. Another country.
Quarter or half turns, some days, smell of damp
and the tape deck. The tape I brought. The spokes
bent and the beat-up tape deck, one bulb,
wobbly rim. The spoke wrench, quarter or half turns,
which pedal threads in reverse. Slowly the rim,
gaps in the spoke lace. At least truer. The grease,
beat-up, the tape I brought back from another
country. Which pedal. Slowly, smell of damp,
some days no-one comes. Kickstands. Quarter
or half, the spokes bent, the tape, at least
truer. Some days, the smell of. One bulb,
the wobbly rim. From another country.

THE WANDERER'S PSALM IN SEARCH OF HOME

If I forget you Jerusalem, let my right hand forget,
Let my tongue be glued to the roof of my mouth if I do not remember you.
If I do not raise Jerusalem up over all my happiness.
—Psalm 137:5-6

i.

From the port, the bus rolls along the Mediterranean until it turns east for the ascent. The road from the coast is, in 1986, a two-lane highway through dry scrub-pine hills and mowed fields. Climbing you pass strategically abandoned armored cars and giant signs of a Hebrew saint's stuttering last words. Around the last bend the first of the many Jerusalems, the expanding, sandstone Jewish city, spreads before you, with the old walled city inside it, the concrete Arab city shadowed behind, and the cloud of the mythic city hanging above.

ii.

I threw a dime into the European fountain
forget, forget my father
Shaved my face too hard while I was counting
forget, forget my home

I cut my hair in the bathroom of a train
to sleep, to sleep my father
Counted sleeper cars with the sound of my name
my father, to sleep in the wind

My guitar protected in something too soft
how can, how can I sing
Kilometers kept washing off
my father's song in a strange land

Tried to agree with the bare sky at least
empty, empty to sleep
Aegean sundown and a ship east
forget, forget my way home

iii.

25 years later the living room floor is littered: plastic rings,
half-chewed board books, soft objects concealing bells. A
few minutes ago she was red and screaming against my
chest; now she babbles, mouths an aqua or canary yellow
ring, and lifts interested blue eyes. The room encloses us
with all the forward pressure of DNA doubling. Above
us, two bedrooms, an insulated attic to trap the heat, and
the common American shingle roof, to keep the rain out.

iv.

I have given my hand away for a visible child
forget or forgive, my father
I may get it back, she looks up—

*If I forget thee, let my right hand
be lost with the left one. If I do not place thee
over all my happiness, let my tongue
shut itself into the box of my mouth.*

v.

Set my pack on the bed. But I had dropped the pocket-knife, somewhere in Austria, or was it the eastern border of France. The gray weight buckled back on my shoulders, I walked and studied the ground while the colors were loosening their hold from small shapes.

And it was cold that evening, and the windbreak trees along the empty field were whirring with blackbirds, or I was hovering along the empty road still pulsing with day heat. But the branches were thick with them. I wanted a story, or, I wanted to know something about home. Getting back to the hostel took hours: whirring on the way, bare field, full trees. All that walking in the dark.

the problem
with sleep
is also

ODE TO I SAID YES

1.
Out of nothing's hollow trunk come the babies, on their
        spongy knees, peering
out of God's back pocket, folded around themselves, full of the
        new air, sponging up color coming in floods,
skin open wide under cleanest white fabric, they come:
recombined are the scattered particles, now emerged and
        perched on branches, fluttering.
Come babies in, from folds on folds of night, of emptywhere
        behind night, the undulating basin of the universe,
just when I thought the door was held closed—latch is sprung,
        bolt thrown,
in come babies, because all they need is cracks.

2.
Babies in the snow, in their disposable diapers, babies racing
        shoreward in kayaks, back from the islands, not content
        to be sequestered in huts,
babies in summer array, in sun-hats, slung from fathers'
        shoulders with bravado, knot craft, buckles and straps.
Babies in the oval office, gumming up the war room, spitting
        up onto strategic maps and Windsor knots:
silk blouses shimmer and spread glad as flags in the morning to
        receive liquids from within the universe's new flowers.
"Mr. President, you have breakfast on your blazer." "Thank
        you, Mr. Secretary, babies will make themselves at
        home."

3.

Babies in catamarans, familiar with buoyancy, flotillas of
     babies carried on the impartial breezes.

Yesterday's babies, tomorrow's world leaders, toddling
     ferociously around the sandbox, laughing at
     gravity, unenchanted with our legacy of rules.

Hallelujah, out of the parted sea come the babies,
     shaking their tambourines, glittering in their
     world-struck eyes,

flying on cotton wings of swaddling cloth, gathering
     size like the avalanche snowball, spilling out onto
     desert ground like a spring squall,

the dry spell broken by the babies, their eyes ready to
     pull mountains, their eyes giant as tractor tires,

it's the end of winter now the season is wail, is suckle
     and sleep, the season is carried tender as membrane
     cradled trembling in your stunned, close arms.

RESOLVING

The sky tells the glory of God, and the heavens speak the works of his hands.
From day to day they say the word and night to night express the thought.
—Psalm 19:2-3

The problem with sleep is also
the absence of God. The skies
which said that word on a daily
basis are gone, and now night has
taken the colors back and left
the blinking of an unset
digital readout. The problem
with sleep is what a baby in this
very house knows, who chases
awake crying almost on the hour
voicing the squall at the base
of speech. O unfriendly windows,
have you also turned your backs
on me, uncurtained blank
expressions pointed out at the long
thin fingers of wind in trees,
or the absence of trees. Catalogues
have come in the mail prepared
page by page with careful human
labor and they too offer
no solution. Once I
rode in a small practical
khaki-hued German car with
my mother through the Nevada
Badlands, striated mounds of stumpy
gnarled stone as I remember
and their statement in the bare
daylight may have explained
the thing about sleep. The windows

of the car of my memory
are smudged and blurring Nevada now,
and the car regardless keeps
moving, its square back full of house
plants receding toward the east and I
think that sleep might rinse them
clean like the blue gas station
fluid but that brings me back
to my problem. I also had a simple shoe
box packed somewhere in the dark
of that car, full of magic tricks
practiced for hours in a room
with no window until I too could make
the ball of sponge disappear
from my fist, my best
trick, it would multiply
into three soft red balls
like juiceless fruits, but none
of those tricks was as good
as sleep. The car's square
back has been crushed and no doubt
stacked in a desolate
yard of flattened steel shells
and the box of tricks is even longer
gone but the erratic or unpredictable
problem of sleep is all around me
tonight, its small hours moving into
or away from each other, just as in
the idea which has always felt
like Nevada to me, that the supposed edges
of the universe are continually going
out away from each other, they
say they know this from
the measured color which shifts
towards red, moving as far into
the future as our minds will go.

DAUGHTER SONGS

With Paul Simon

I am always thinking about time:
the fluid or pool where our minds swim. Like if I see trees, it was
the other tree I saw, or the wind hissing through them, and what
I want to say the wind says better. Take, for instance, a time
the Stevie Wonder song from 1972 comes on, and dissolves on the tongue as if it was
a filo dough of his voices and supple Rhodes chords layered one at a time
from every point in your life you ever heard it—his surge of innocence,
I love I love I love I love every little thing about you, can you locate a time
it stands still, by itself, not pouring backwards and forwards its stream of confidences?

And doesn't everything that sweet feel like long ago,
like echoes, caught in the honey trap of the past? As if it must
leave before it has arrived. But arrive you have, who still belong
to yourself, looking up surprised as I come or go,
straining away from my memories, towards you. Lifting you when you wake, I have
no container for that feeling, the new skin, the climbing onto me; the photograph
won't hold this. So we slough after you, in our frazzle to preserve your
small unblemished body from blunt things. Yes but the memories, they're
already mounding up around you, and who has a shovel, and finally all that's
in my hands is a song, chorusing back through the leaving and the left,
which I'm carrying, for any chance to sing you.

DEVOTION

I don't love you as much as I love sleep.

Sleep has left me for someone who will treat it better.

Tried to blow out the candles until breathless. Guess what my wish was.

Let me take you to a hollow where the kids go get high & make out. It's
    quiet there.

When I drank sleep too fast I burned my tongue.

I saw you go into the minimart & come out only with one tin of mints. But
    I was driving, as I always am. Too fast.

When we wake up, how about we renew our vows? With my eyes closed I
    say I don't love anyone.

In the tiny place where I lay me down, the problem of breathing.

You left the station with half a tank for a full night of sleep.

I under-tongued melatonin, looked for the white place phasing between
    headphones. Not drinking, no more birthdays.

Pandemonium at the big-box store, where they're running a special on
    sleep.

I started saying I don't love you, but I was lying.

Even here, in heavy rains with the blinds down, while everyone hurries in
    channels carved by money: head buried, nothing to lose but sleep.

I can't be awake the way I want to, he said to his phone when it
said 3 am. Outside, even the cars were trying to.

Don't rush me while I try to arrive at the word which has been on
every mother's lips since the first evening.

While they page, drape their attention across the headlines: the
color that ripples through there is sleep.

Sleep's picture on the back of the milk carton, still missing.

But probably it isn't sleep that I'm missing, it's you.

The only time I'm not lying.

I'd be lying if I said I didn't love you. My face in the dark.

LABOR POEM #12

Bette's Ocean View Diner, Berkeley CA

Though I lied, the chef's knife, staccato, green
stains or red stains. The off-white cutting board. From
the stack of aprons, hand towels, all white to start.
Snap peas. The curled line of fingernails. I lied
at the interview, chef's knife rocking, fancy
ham, or red stains. Snap peas blanched, then julienned.
To start, from the aprons waist-tied, hand towel
tucked. The off-white, ten-inch chef's knife, fingernails,
finally. All white from the stack though I
lied about my experience. Green stains
or red, staccato along the curled line.
Finally the acrid bleach. Fancy ham, waist-
tied, from the stack to start all white. Rocking on
its point. My experience. Blanched, julienned.

HELPLESS

Once again Neil Young from the sundown
glow around 1970   my spirit then
being coated gray   one vacant room

at a time   *Blue windows behind the stars*

Everyone is gone   Morning
sun past bare branch
& power line   slant-shadows
the front window muntins

Across synapses the widened
young sense world calls
to this one   three chords turning
in the rise and fall   of which apparently we

are also made   I can see many
envelopes piled with tri-
folded worries   civilization as

a refrigerator grrs bringing along
for us   leftovers in glass

In my mind   waver
of man-soprano arches
into the fadeout   Four part

ghost of song why do you cling

Does quantum physics help us
they say   a particle goes
to meet anti-particle where one

annihilates the other   or put
otherwise two aspects of one

particle loop   in time

At the shiva yesterday B
who once made a place for me
like sun-light   lingered

by me as long as I could bear
wearing out   while the mourner went on
about his father   My father

tells me my sister in her next
facility   doesn't lift

her head to see he's there

FROM MY FATHER TRANSLATING FREELY TO US OUT OF HIS HAND-HELD HEBREW BIBLE, I ONLY RECALL ONE STORY

Two times Samson
the only real
hero for a boy in a book full
of men with sky
in their mouths & second
sons threading the future
out of their brothers'
air   fell for a woman
of the other side
& it was always
crops torched   bride
burned until there he was
in his fist a donkey's jawbone

When I look at you tonight
bay faded into a dim
suggestion   & your eyes
I know to be a blue from a distance
I never get used to
but now no color & pooled
with joy at the tinsel
pastels arching up their
surprise from the other shore
          I wonder at how men's
imagination of a woman leads us
out from our cramped
huts of selves until
in some far house we will
only ask for strength
in the darkness not to pull it
all down on top of us

LABOR POEM #17

Life Safety System Crew

The campus is celebrating the opening of the $162.3 million Stanley Hall...
[an] 11 story building, three floors of which are below ground... The exterior
... is clad in Sierra white granite and copper...
—UC Berkeley press release, September 2007.

The face around his eyes: Eric, Dave, maybe
an 8 foot ladder. All-job safety, bull-horn, in front.
Hundreds of us for the bull-horn meetings.
My journeyman. Maybe an 8 footer,
they were talking, Ryan. In the front, to be *clad*
in Sierra white granite and copper. On
my shoulder, Eric, Dave, the face around. "I
think I'll call you Kosher boy," Ryan, smiling.
Hundreds of us in front, for the bull-horn.
And copper. Talking about me, when I charged
down, the face around his eyes got wide. Down
the hall, they were, all-job safety, maybe
a ladder on my shoulder, Kosher, when I
charged. Eric, *Sierra white.* Eyes got wide.

EYES WE THINK WE KNOW SO WELL

With Bob Dylan

New territory, chance of rain, I ride
until I can't & then walk the rest of the way on
the water. But they don't see my miracle, only a mail train
that rattles past. Just like the big eyes of a baby can't
say what's in her head, no matter how you look. Won't buy
glasses that can read those thoughts. Wanted a thrill

but today's not too lucky, like a lottery ticket I've been
scratching bare. Chance goes up, clouds all
conspire down on the nannies, the night baby
who made it to morning. Now the rain, slanting in, leaning on,
streaking windows, saturating the windowsill. Well

lie down in a doorway, worried if I die on
the inside of my dream, then no rest. All bottom, no top,
better keep climbing. Tired of climbing, tired of the hill,

tired of my feet in shoes, and if I
stop climbing I'm nowhere. They don't make
a life story the way they used to. Shuffle, you know
it's still the same 52. While I deal my baby
is looking, up at me, wonder if she always will.

1970'S MARIN, IMAGINED AS A COME-ON

Oh ropy scent of burning marijuana,
carved jade in Caucasian chest skin
made leathery, top down along the coastal road
from fog to forever, will you take me to marinate
in your redwood hot tub under totem Mt. Tam,
its spirit gong bronzing all day past the industrial
fairy-arches of the Golden Gate beckoning to Asia
with open shipping lanes & suicide in a whisper?
Be my raw sugar daddy, lay your dollar
on my dollar. We can deal our children
face down, we can fold em,
oo I like that adrenaline buzz. For you
my hair is blonde; make love to me lavishly,
like we learned in the seminars, take me
on a mantra-powered ride down my chakras
to the volcanic core. Read me
the runes through your rabbi-eyes.
All my greatest bands are dead,
so hold my bone-handled bread knife
& slice again: I want to be as whole
as that loaf & I want to be cut open
& spread with something
sunny, something Morocco
& peasant & five stars all at once.
Yes fuck me like we've escaped Hollywood
& we're coming to take it back.
Fuck me like Hendrix covering Dylan,
like the Stones covering Hendrix, like Dylan
covered in whiteface on the Rolling Thunder tour.
Cover me with thunder. I have sat
lotused in the Zendo long enough.
Take me to the flea market, we're almost

free: tie dye, god's eyes, sand candles,
nothing on under my Andes poncho.
Now that all we have left
is our flesh, it's time to carve into it.

YOUR ROOM

for G. C. A.

Then you were dating Neil Young's
daughter, which she turned out not

to be, but you kept trying to
write her a song and that song

turned back on itself halfway,
keys softened off their notes and I

lost track as here we got even
busier, bought a house and ripped

the walls open. On my playlist
Neil will always rise and dip

with the pedal steel swells, tires
rolling through a long dark Al-

bu-querque, high, that molasses
sadness, the harmonica's high

slurred crying, and we don't even
like to get high but would be

so happy to lean into
those chords. I know it didn't

work out with you and Neil
Young's not-daughter, she needed

more pursuit than your second
guessing would allow. Which leaves

your Brooklyn cereal bowl and key-
board room too small, not that I

am romance's prime instance,
still I want you to reach

the end of your day with some
one kind, near. Neil, like our

sister, has seizures, so he's
seen the same cleaved absenting

of time but from the in-
side, bright broken lines. Not

to say her mind's trapdooring
dented your world the same as

mine, a hole where those closest
to me fall, but that if I

could build a house like a house
was meant, I'd make a room where

your songs are framed right into
the walls, and us there singing

WATCHING MY FAMILY IN THE DARK, THE WRONG SONG IN MY HEAD

Oceans of time, but we are poor
swimmers. In their armada
around us the night hours
are sailing. *Your mother says*
that I'm a stranger, sustains the man
in the bluegrass. Nonetheless
I know you in loose pajamas
worn thin, the fuzzy this and that
socks you will be shedding
as you sleep. *I*
am a man of constant sorrow,
sadness I've been around
so long I don't even notice
it ringing. Around the ninth
hour of pushing we crouched
down, your back pouring off sweat
in my hands while you fought
her out, a surprise blood
pool on the floor and the midwives
calling out the heartbeat.

Swimmers who can only go
one way, we warm
in the last of a sun we don't
feel safe in. Now
the tide of dishes, torn open
window envelopes, yard
matted again with bindweed.
Her small snoring
into the increasingly unstable
weather, so many ways

to worry until morning, tiny
currents across light
emitting diodes subtract
a spot of dark from the book,
my loyal one, you keep
holding as always trying
not to fall out
of the day. But you made
us this one with all
its little breaths.

POEM

I think about sex when I'm going to sleep.
We've said last words: the work day
waits with its blades whirring;
and then I think about sex, old sex, vague
echoed sex, a fragment of sliding inside
someone, no face or colors.
So many memories for the mind
to page but when I go to sleep I think
of some unvivid bit of body touching
body, as if the thumb was tucked
back in the mouth, before slipping
out in night's thin canoe—
you are already off quiet
on the current, while I linger on a few
frames where the star is the pelvises
pulsing together, the warm and the wet,
all those forgotten molecules of the wild
weird real thing boiled down to this
flashlighted snapshot of fucking, it comes
back like that, aftermath, spinning
reel-whirr and flicker of old
machinery, popping, caught.

LABOR POEM #16

Lafayette Electric, Redwood City, CA

Against the pour and set of concrete, four flung feet of the A-frame.
Palm-sweat. The fiberglass rails, steps, my reach in ducts and shadows. The four
feet spread across silica piled, steel debris. Rotohammer snarl.
My waist, up through the tangle of ceiling wires, a few extra inches.

The steady, the rubber-butted feet. Everywhere a film of dust. Up
in shadows, waist above, flimsy of T-bar steel, and somewhere, windows.
The fiberglass steady, aluminum and spread of the 8-footer,
extra inches, and the snarl among trunks of duct, cables spidered

away. If a few more inches of reach, in spidered shadows above
the grid, and daylight removed from window-banks. And the ladder feet freed,
from four dusty stations. Over the pour and set, its steady and scrap
piles. My reach, above the screen of daylight somewhere, the fall of palm-

sweaty while the freedom of fiberglass, loose of aluminum, as
my reach to the twistable, flimsy grid, swinging down, out of duct
trunks and tangle from a high step of the 8 footer, swinging low
to the station of concrete. Windows removed daylight, somewhere away.

NOT PORTLAND

for D.S.

When was
                        the last time
          I'm hoping not Portland
                        Wind glitters the new
                              grass & rain
                  has mud-ponded
          a horse trail
                        in what passes
              for winter here   half
                    spring   I throw word
            crumbs into the no
                              where you were

                                                  At the funeral N
remembered   that summer   how
                        to camp where we sang one
                        union   shall   & raised the blue
                              on white   star
you brought a pamphlet
              Marx's answer
                      to the Jews   you found
          funny   chorusing
                              We Germans
                              are not free how
                        can we free you

Are you free now
                              is that
          what this means

Dead end of Belgium Trail

FOR YOU (A BOOK ABOUT US)

What does sun going have to do with us? From street
       & spruce it withdraws, leaving us rooms full of
       leaving. Or trying not to.

What would I be able to say, were my shoulders covered
       with sparrows. Jays, I know those. They're bluer.

I've been working on a book between us, one I'm
       putting everything in.

What if us is more beautiful than, than what.

Can we tell? Both trying to stay in the bluest part of the
       flame. You can't not be let down: I find

somewhere farther. Pines fade to italics, daylight
       minused. From my station down the hall
       sometimes the sound of you breathing.

In the near past, thin-sliced, in another language I know,
       in a ballad passed down and handled to a shine,
       would those words come closer.

Overwhelmed sunset we run a wire through, from some
       turbine out of sight.

Not the sunset we don't ride into. Harder in the dark not
       to be confused.

I go to make up my mind but there's another wire. To
       trip. Between poles of want & going.

Do these things always come back? Night window
saying absence. A camera in your hand.

& twenty years of time lapse: patience, not as easy to
register for as tableware.

In the window a table-lamp floats close to stairs. Always
stairs, leading to the other day,

in a language one of us doesn't know where I love you
wasn't a bird I never learned the name for

flying away. You are not listening is a song I know.

By sorrow heart. Yard full of weeds are you still
listening? Not only weeds: our outrageous rose-
bush, orange elephant-lilies over our heads.

I'm writing a book about songs between us, like rope
ladders over a fissure.

Falling off to my half-night, send me that picture I'll
take it along. Is this a one-click, or does it go
between?

I'm writing a book where we stare at each other through
megapixels. I'm keeping my pictures folded in
this screen, how thin. I'm wearing shoes made of
apologies. I'm walking towards you. Birdsongs
& blue pages that fall out of absence where the
sky was.

In the old ballad the king pleading brings gifts, they each
contain fifty silver bells & ten. Something about
love.

I love that ballad, it's a Child. I want to bring its bells to
you.

A book that explains how I love is a prayer. If one of us
prayed.

Is another day.

I'll be a book, at your bedside always. You'll be always,
not wanting it to end.

& ON HE FLARED

                wrote John unfinishing
his final big thing, in his own eyes
failing. What can I get started for you
asks the barista into a blink of blue light
while Tom Petty jingle jangles
also gone. Once David arrived with somehow
Ben in tow, to minivan us from there to Baja. *Again
you ring the memories' doorbell?* What else

do I have? Tom in the dash
the length of Californias, Free
Falling anthemed us like the wheels
we are always on. *No matter
how many years load between you
and them.* Or death. Another time
it was Ben on the phone, David & his bus
had gathered into an oncoming pickup
somewhere two-laned & farther than I

could have imagined. *Don't the friends
stand in for your family, perforations
like cracker pieces as each was broken off?*
They were going to be my real family.
So you were betrayed again. I suppose
by time. John Keats I meant to keep
your line going past where you stopped
at Memory resting, as a sun god's flames

startled away birds which were hours.
But I was never much for the Greek gods,
their oiled biceps, fucking & contending.

Quiet in the back seat Peter
seemed most like my own soul—
which part of that murk are you calling
soul? Which part of the past flares on
in a cafe that repeats everywhere

like money. The sun hitting thin top
of David's twenty years ago Toyota
has exchanged for one that weather-beats
his memory in Ben's mind & mine
& the someone's Peter is now.
Behind your face weren't you
usually crumbling? Right, the broken
cracker. In a cafe, I flicker
with envy for poor blood-coughing

Keats oh so dead, but his lines
still vibrating. Apollo has followed
Hyperion into imagination's
scrap heap. *Which you root in.*

We tried to lie down for the night
by sounds of surf. But panicked
back into the van from the barks
of wild dogs which in the morning
were mutts behind a rag-tag
barn-fence. *Chasing imagination backward.*

Doesn't it chase us? *That's not imagination.*
My abandoned poem to the friend
who is no longer Peter ended:
                            Oh memory,
we try to break free. *So it's really about endings.*
Where I begin—something unfinished—

RISE UP MY FRIEND MY LOVELY ONE

(Song of Songs 2:13)

                    In the finale
of the Trolley Dances our daughter
& I watched harnessed women pendulum
& loft in lime green sunglasses
high over a Hunter's Point
sidewalk. But without much
kissing lately the days stop
& go taillighting like the cars
on 580 East Friday at five.
We worry, a constant mental
coughing, medicine lost
in the closet's apocalypse. & sun

rides rear windshields as
in a gleaming limitless line
the city unloads its day's labor
over the Altamont toward the feasible
valley housing, *rise up my friend*
my lovely one and come away.
                        Who is there
to blame? But the flicker of signals
through water & a few carbons
that constitutes my self dragging
from a finally empty kitchen sink
over clothes & Lego remnants to mattress
at last. Was this how an ancestor felt
through months of stone
walled rain before he uttered
his verse?
                Which we spoke years
ago as among a hum of witnesses

we circled each other doing
all words can to tie a life
to a life. What line between
that night & this? Days that inch
away, dancers suspended
from a wall with slight smiles as they
somersault off the vertical face of it.

SILENCES OF ISAAC

& how am I after all these years a father
when I wake up   Rain not falling   pollen drifts
the city   settling over what I can't say

A bus sighs past   The clematis has climbed
my neighbor's roof all night   Its silence reminds me
of calling all morning but can't get through

The strategies of ants too come down to this
way one continues within the many & I
got up early enough to still not say it

Humans squandered in increments of stop & go
Mold whitens   shrivels leaves of what is that tree
called   each   suspended as daylight arrives

What could Isaac say after the machine of that

story used him   Some silence is not God it's just
being locked up in your head   Before dawn our

ancestors are already working   In that
version Ishmael   this one Isaac   Either way
a shrug   stone-colored footsteps   the sun coming up

ACKNOWLEDGEMENTS

The following poems have been published in the journals indicated:

"16 Arlosoroff," *Squaw Valley Review* 2014

"1970's Marin, imagined as a come-on," *Court Green #20,* 2021

"America, Proposal," *Museum of Americana #20,* 2020

"Daughter Songs," *Squaw Valley Review,* 2011

"Devotion," *Random Sample #4,* 2020

"Fog Over Ashkenaz," *Arkana* 9, December 2020

"Gates," *Field,* Spring 2015

"I was also one of the Boys of Summer," *Assembly* 2011

"Jerusalem, From Increasing Distances," *Zeek* 2009

"Labor Poem (Wisconsin State Journal)," Labor Poem (Subway Guitars Bicycles)": *Juke Joint 4,* November 2018

"Labor Poem (Banana Plantation)," *Squaw Valley Review,* 2011

"Labor Poem (Fonseca Construction)" Zyzzyva 100 Spring 2014

"Labor Poem (Tractor Delivery)," *Fourteen Hills 20.2,* Spring 2014

"Labor Poem (Lafayette Electric)," *Newfound,* Fall 2014

"Labor Poem (Polyziv)," *Paper Nautilus,* Fall 2013

"Labor Poem (Student Services newsletter)," *PANK* 12.1, Fall/Winter 2016

"Labor Poem (Life Safety System Crew), " *Star82*, March 2018

"Ode to growing up ten years too late," *Court Green #20,* 2021

"Ode to I said Yes," *Limehawk,* Spring 2015

"Ode to my lost virginity," *Book of Matches #2,* 2021

"Ode to the Idea of France," *Field,* Spring 2017

"Poem with dishes & dead sea," *Written Here,* 2018
"Resolving," *Burnside Review,* Spring 2015
"Silences of Isaac," *Pretty Owl Poetry,* January 2019
"Tomatoes: Summer's First," *The Cafe Review,* Fall 2013
"Your Room," *Zyzzyva,* Winter 2015
"Walking by the lake after studying Torah," *Coal Hill Review* Fall 2019

NOTES

Gratitude: to all the poets whose forms and methods I cribbed, borrowed and/or stole. The most blatant: Joshua Beckman for the sonnettish template of the "Labor Poems;" Terrance Hayes for his beloved Golden Shovel ("Daughter Songs," "America, Proposal," and "Eyes we think we know so well"); Robert Bly for the tercet ghazal which scaffolded a number of ghazalesque poems here. To Brenda Hillman, Mathew Zapruder and my fellow poets at Saint Mary's College of California where I wrote and learned so much. To staff and participants of the Community of Writers at Olympic Valley, poetry heaven, where many of these were drafted. To my loyal and generous readers, particularly Ross Belot, Sara Burant, Daniel Schifrin, Elliot Schain, and Chris Wilson, who looked at so many of these over the years. To Arisa White, Tess Taylor, Yakir Ben-Moshe, Geoffrey O'Brien, Forrest Gander, Cathy Park Hong, Major Jackson, Alan Shapiro, Juliana Spahr, and many other poets who have offered support and friendship. To my parents for their support. To Gaby Alter, who keeps his faith in me. To Jess and Hadas for giving me a house full of life and love to come back to after I've gone climbing peaks or digging holes to find these poems.

"Gates" contains lines from a poem [*sha'ar p'takh dodi*] by Shlomo Ibn Gabirol, one of the greatest of the medieval Hebrew poets of Muslim Spain. Translations from this and other Hebrew texts (with the exception of the excerpt by A.D. Gordon) are mine.

"A Night at the Old Marketplace," a Yiddish play written by I.L. Peretz, was staged by Benjamin Zuskin, lead actor, and Solom Mikhoels, director, of the Moscow State Jewish Theater. This theater, established shortly after the Russian Revolution of 1917, was the world's only state-sponsored Yiddish theater until it was shut down and Zuskin and Mihoels killed in a purge by Stalin in 1952.

Aaron David Gordon was a leading figure of Labor Zionism in the early part of the 20th Century, a writer and elder statesman of the "religion of labor." He was an inspiration to young people whom he lived and worked among in the early years of socialist Jewish settlement in Palestine, and to many of us in the Labor Zionist youth movement *Habonim Dror ("Builders of Liberation")*. Several of the poems in the "Ode to Uprising" series are set in Habonim Camp Tavor, near Three Rivers, Michigan. *Uprising* was the final studio album by Bob Marley and the Wailers.

"Helpless" quotes the CSNY song of that name; "Your room" refers to the Neil Young song "Albuquerque" from his wonderful *Tonight's the Night* album. "*And on he flared*" is the final half-line of John Keat's last unfinished epic poem "The Fall of Hyperion;" the form of my poem owes a debt to Robert Hass's "Berkeley Eclogue."

"Rise up my friend my lovely one" is my translation of a line from *Song of Songs 2:13*. The Altamont is a windmill-studded pass on a highway that leads from the San Francisco Bay Area to cities and towns of the inland San Fernando Valley where many workers are able to afford their homes; the Trolley Dances is an annual modern dance event in San Francisco.